Colors with Bella Lee

By Sasha Dixon

Sasha S. Dixon, Author and artist, from Cleveland Heights, OH. Currently a student majoring in Studio Art at The University Of Akron. Author of *Charm and Passion*, *123 with Bella Lee, Let's explore our ABC's with Bella Lee and Colors with Bella Lee;* developed a love for education after becoming a mother.
Email - sasha.dixon.sd@gmail.com
Facebook - @sashadixon19
Twitter - @SashaDixon19
Instagram - @sashadixon19

This publication is dedicated to Bella Lee and Dr. Martin Luther King Jr.

Skyler S. Warren, Graphic Artist designer of the cover of *Charm and Passion*, illustrator for *123 with Bella lee, Lets explore our ABC's with Bella Lee, and Colors with Bella Lee* Skyler finds passion in working as a graphic designer and illustrator. Helping others while creating smiles wherever he goes.
Email: skylerswarren@gmail.com
Website: http://www.skylerswarren.com

ISBN 978-0692075012

Library of Congress Control Number:

Printed in the United States of America February 2018

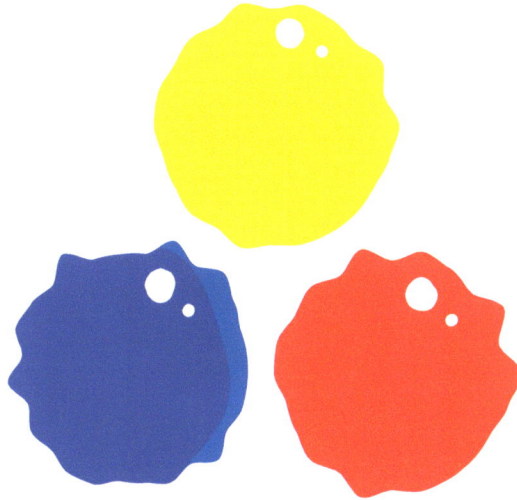

Primary Colors

(prahy-mer-ee kuhl-ers)

Yellow

Blue

Red

A primary color is a color that cannot be made from a combination of any other colors. There are three primary colors **blue**, **yellow** and **red**. These three colors are hues that in theory can be mixed to make all other colors. A hue is the specific look or pigment of a color.

If you mix three primary colors blue, yellow and red.
In theory it will produce black.

This is a red apple.

These are the words, red apple.

RED APPLE

Bella is driving a red car.

This is a blue fish.

These are the words, blue fish.

BLUE FISH

Bella is painting a blue fish.

This is a yellow sun.

These are the words, yellow sun.

YELLOW SUN

Bella saw a yellow bus, during the spring.

Secondary Colors

(sek-uh n-der-ee kuhl-ers)

Orange

Violet   Green

There are three secondary colors violet, orange, and green.
By mixing two primary hues together you will produce
a secondary color.

By mixing red and blue together you will create the color violet.

RED
(Primary)

BLUE
(Primary)

VIOLET
(Secondary)

RED
(Primary)

YELLOW
(Primary)

ORANGE
(Secondary)

By mixing red and yellow together you will create the color orange.

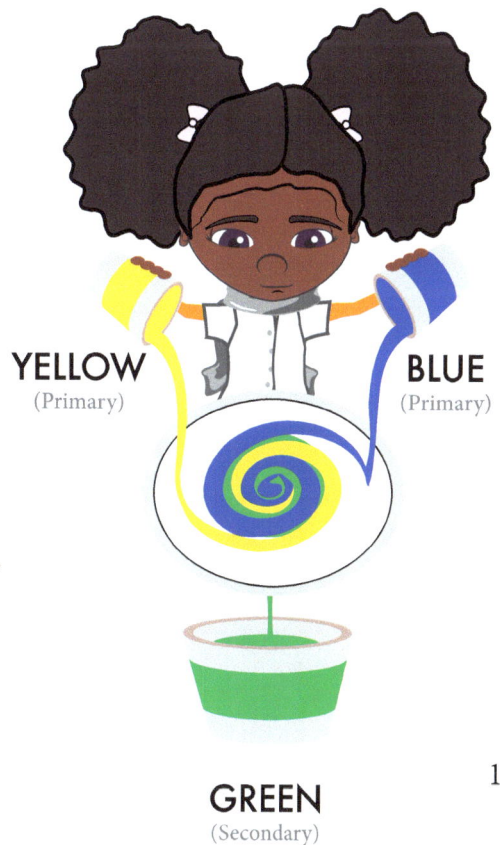

YELLOW
(Primary)

BLUE
(Primary)

By mixing yellow and blue together you will create the color green.

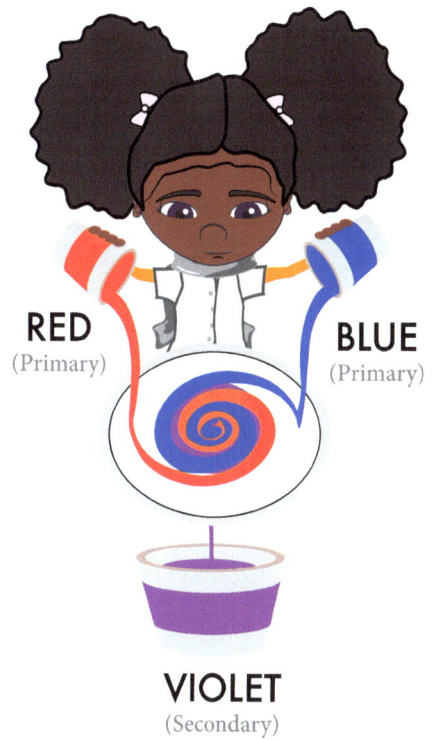

19

GREEN
(Secondary)

This is a orange pumpkin.

These are the words, orange pumpkin.

ORANGE PUMPKIN

Bella is picking a big orange pumpkin for her Halloween costume this year.

This is a violet shoe.

These are the words, violet shoe.

VIOLET SHOE

Bella is wearing her violet shoes at her concert with the chickadee choir.

Peep
Peep
Peep
Peep
Peep
Peep
Peep

This is a green leaf.

These are the words, green leaf.

GREEN LEAF

Bella is watching the green leaves fall from the tree.

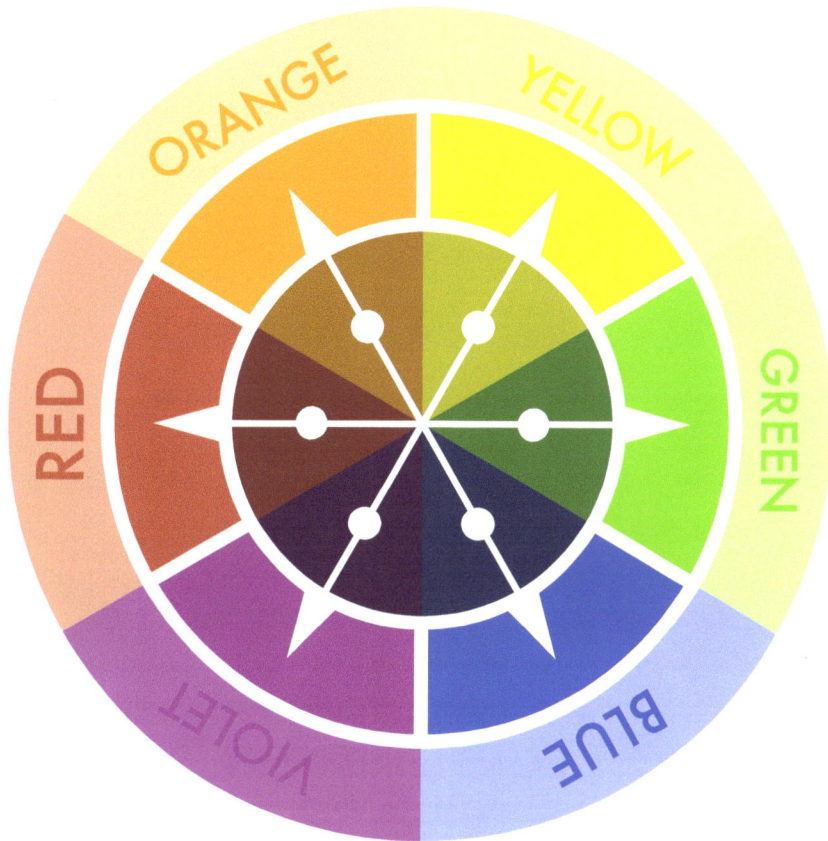

Complimentary Colors

Complimentary colors are colors that are opposite of each other on the color wheel. Complementary colors compliment each other.

This is an example of a color wheel that displays complementary colors.

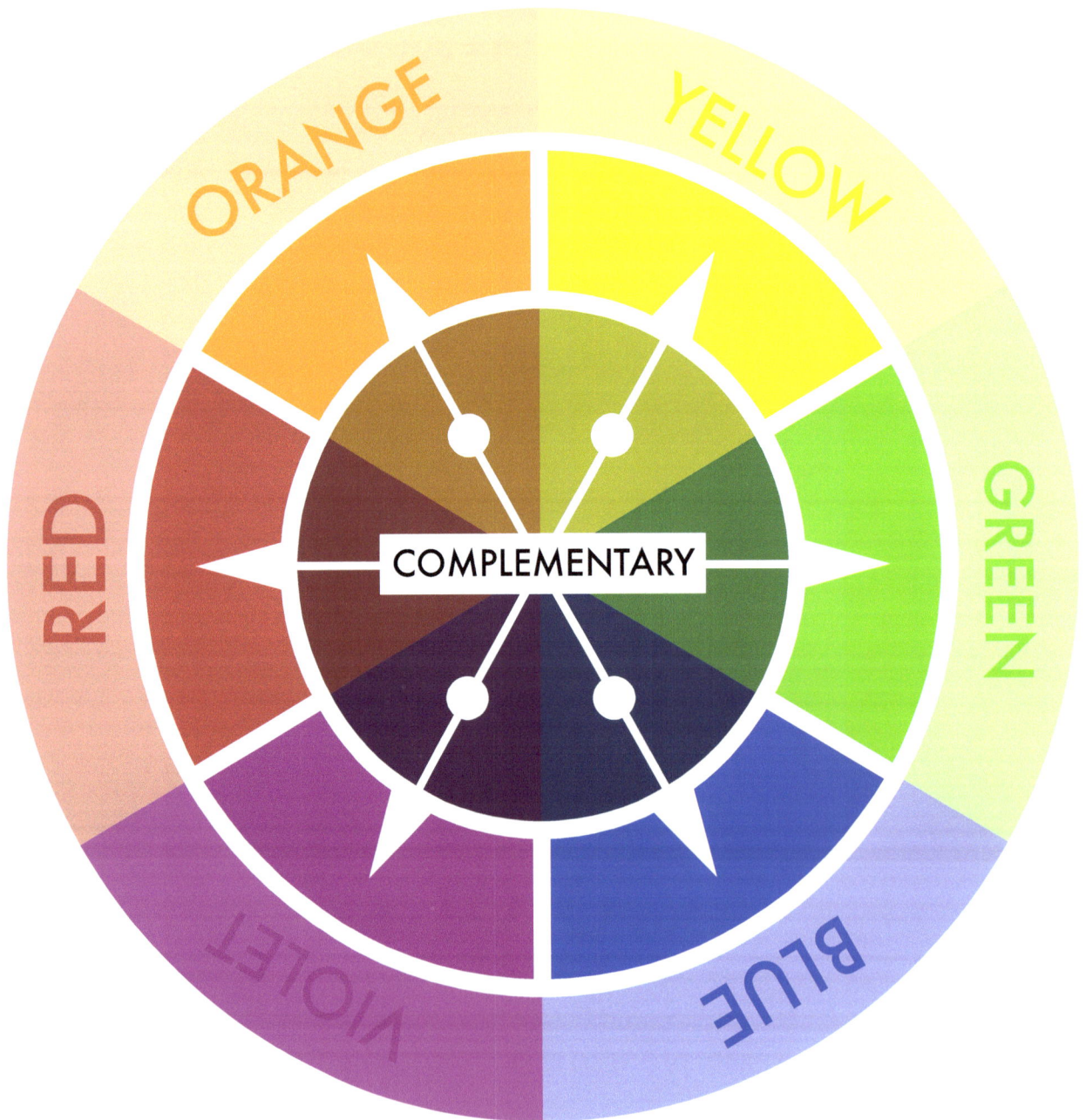

R-O-Y-G-B-V is the order in which artist prepare colors to paint on their paint pallet.

Red and green are colors that compliment one another. Look! Bella is putting a red candy cane on a green christmas tree.

Orange and blue are colors that compliment
each other. Bella is looking at her reflection
in the shiny blue and orange Christmas ornament.

You are very pretty.

I like your stripes!

Yellow and violet are colors that compliment one another.

Thank you!

You smell nice.

The yellow bee is dancing with the violet flower.

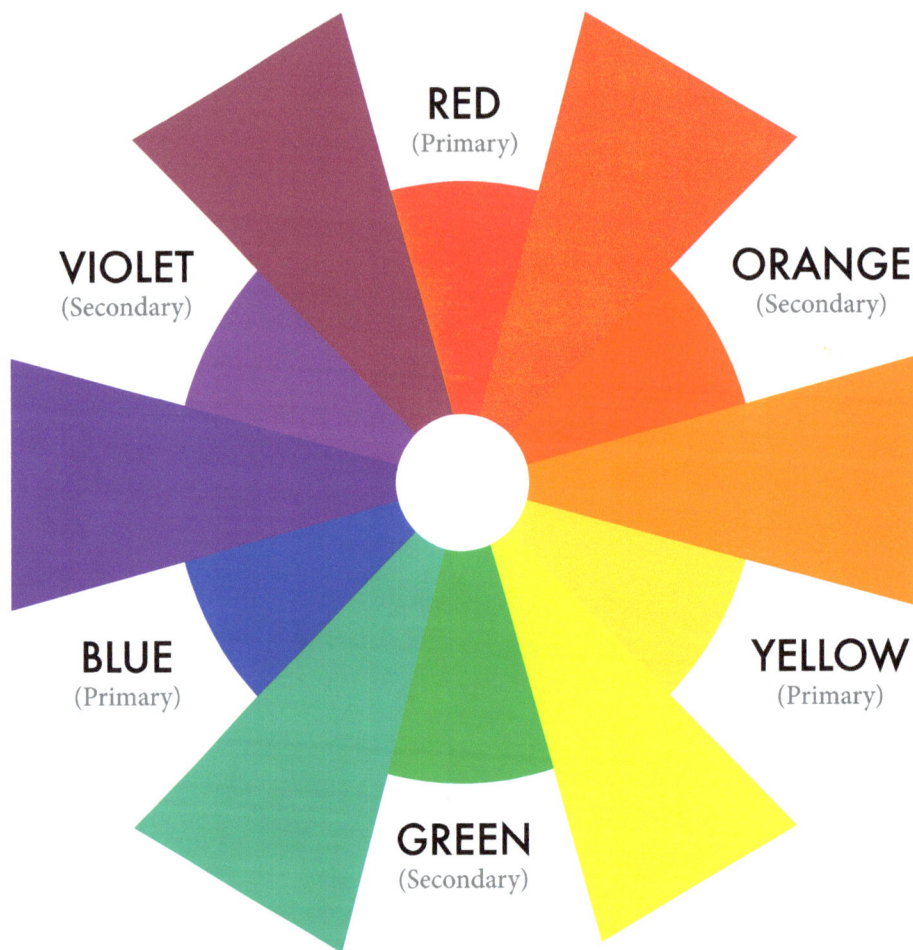

RED
(Primary)

ORANGE
(Secondary)

VIOLET
(Secondary)

YELLOW
(Primary)

BLUE
(Primary)

GREEN
(Secondary)

Tertiary
(tur-shee-er-ee)

Tertiary colors are made by mixing a primary color
and a secondary color together.

By mixing red and violet together you will create the color red-violet.

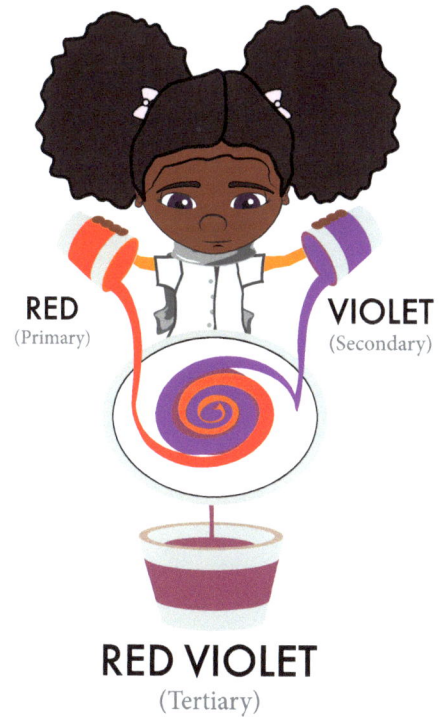

RED
(Primary)

VIOLET
(Secondary)

RED VIOLET
(Tertiary)

RED
(Primary)

ORANGE
(Secondary)

By mixing red and orange together you will create the color red-orange.

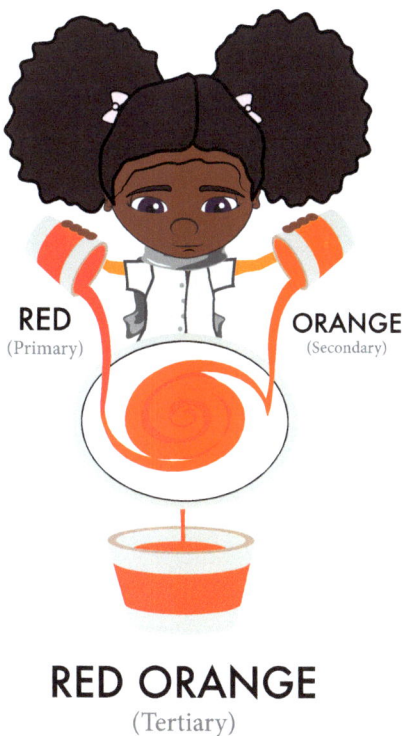

RED ORANGE
(Tertiary)

YELLOW
(Primary)

ORANGE
(Secondary)

By mixing yellow and orange together you will create the color yellow-orange.

YELLOW ORANGE
(Tertiary)

By mixing blue and violet together you will create the color blue-violet.

BLUE
(Primary)

VIOLET
(Secondary)

BLUE VIOLET
(Tertiary)

By mixing yellow and green together you will create the color yellow-green.

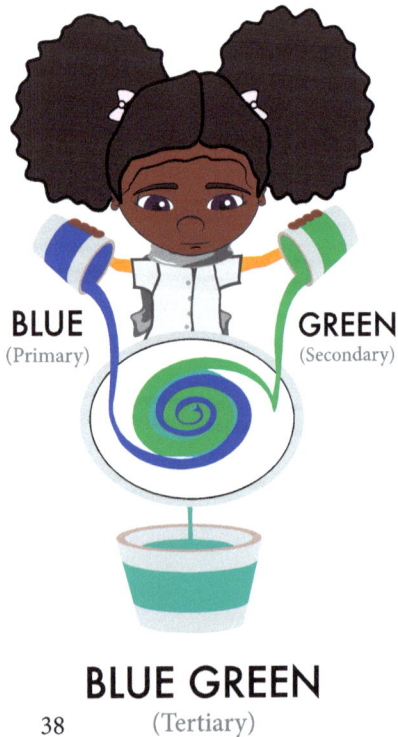

YELLOW
(Primary)

GREEN
(Secondary)

YELLOW GREEN
(Tertiary)

BLUE
(Primary)

GREEN
(Secondary)

By mixing blue and green together you will create the color blue-green.

BLUE GREEN
(Tertiary)

RED + **ORANGE** = **RED ORANGE**

YELLOW + **ORANGE** = **YELLOW ORANGE**

YELLOW + **GREEN** = **YELLOW GREEN**

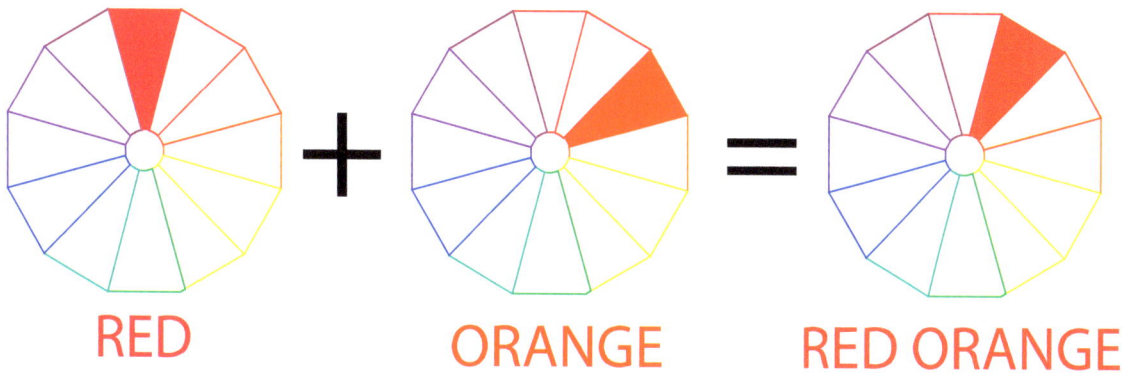

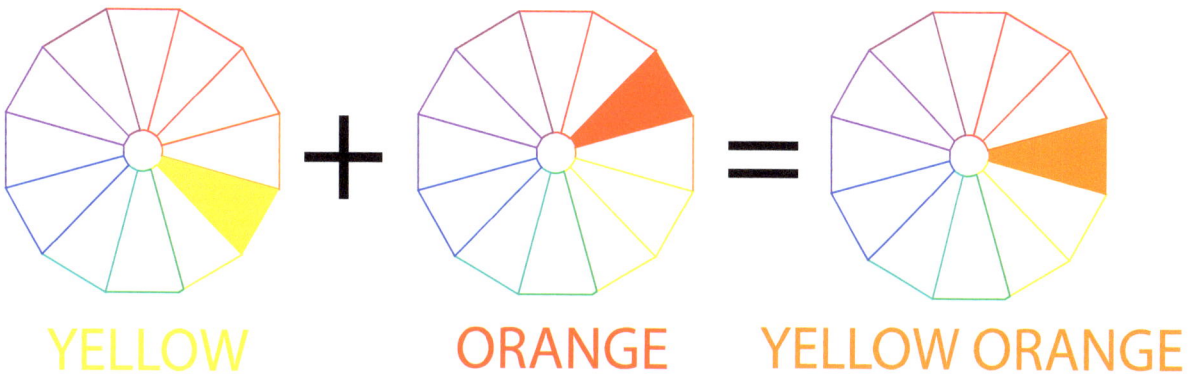

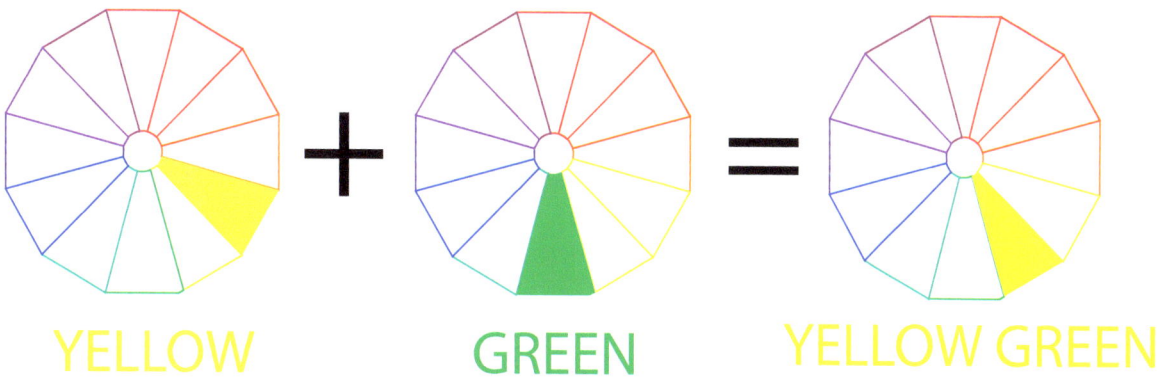

Here are formulas that are used to create tertiary colors.

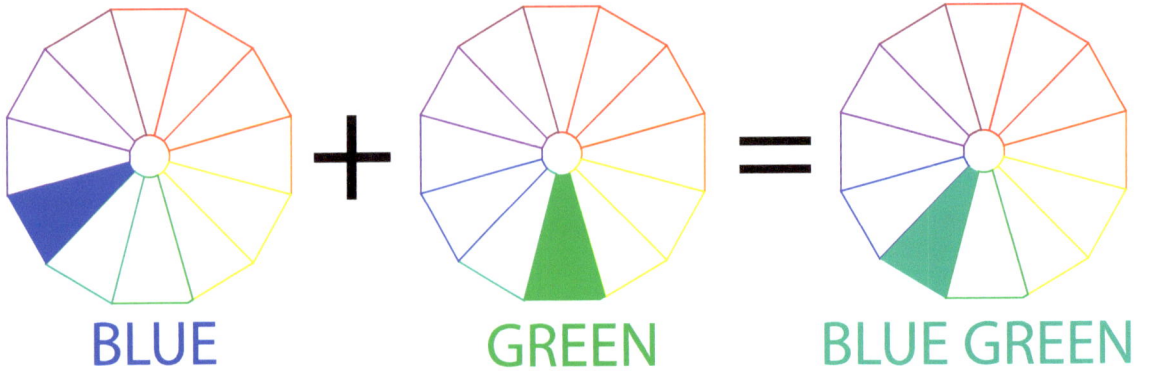

BLUE + **GREEN** = **BLUE GREEN**

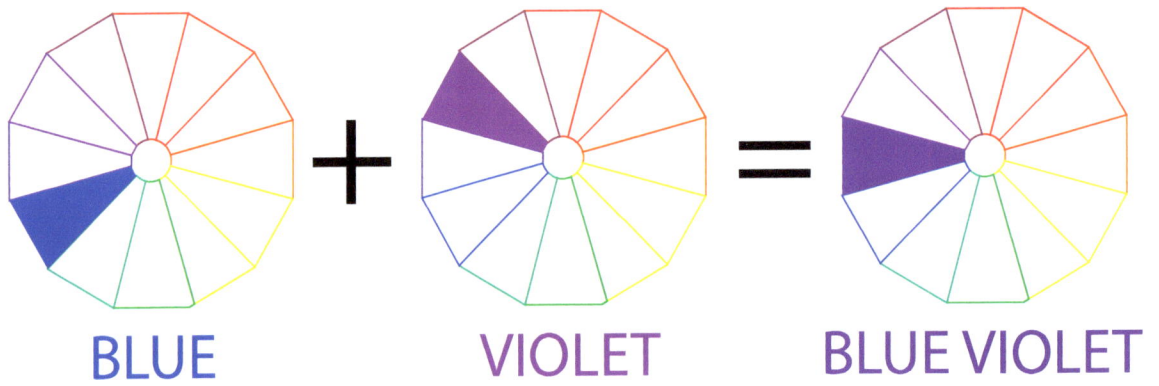

BLUE + **VIOLET** = **BLUE VIOLET**

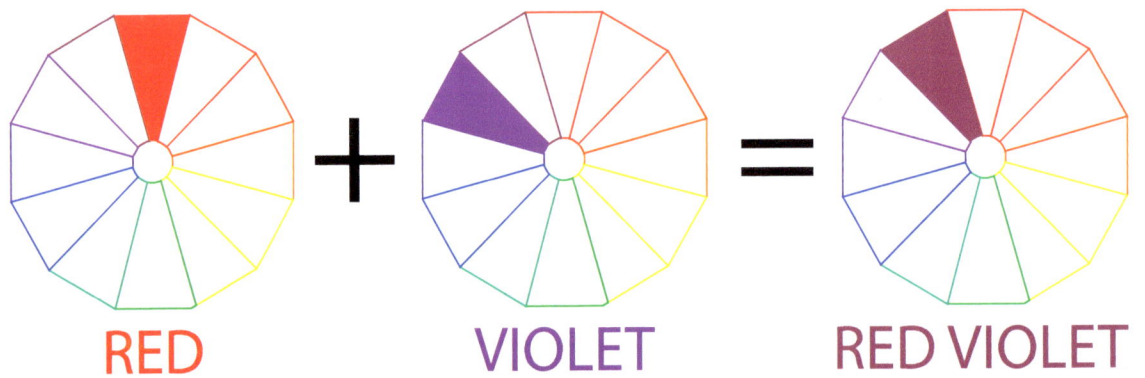

RED + **VIOLET** = **RED VIOLET**

This is a blue-green crayon.

This is a red-orange crayon.

This is a blue-violet crayon.

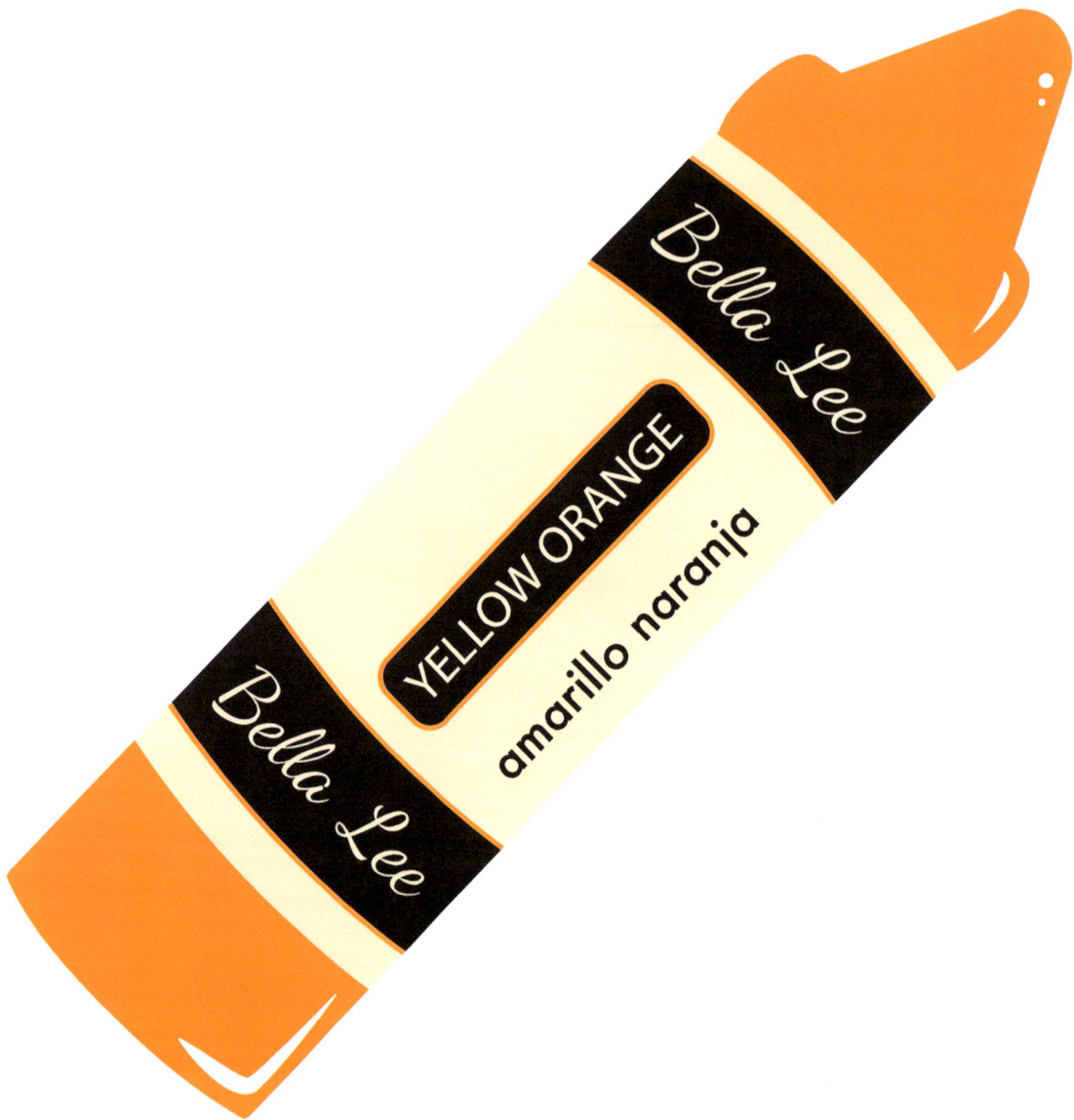

This is a yellow-orange crayon.

Bella Lee

RED VIOLET

violeta rojizo

Bella Lee

This is a red-violet crayon.

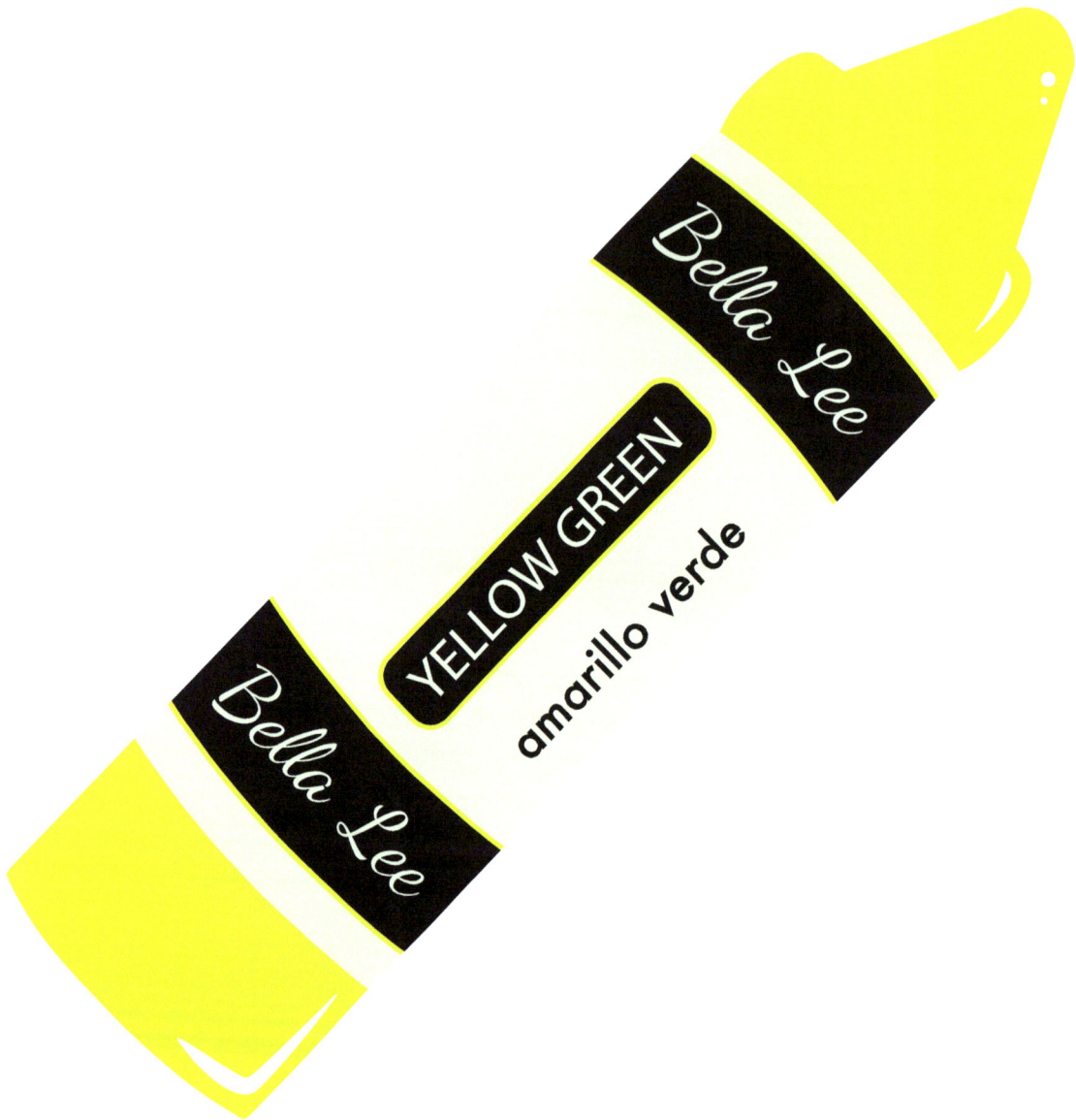

This is a yellow-green crayon.

Bye bye!

Recommended editions:
123 with Bella Lee,
Lets explore our ABC's with Bella Lee.
More editions coming soon.

www.ingramcontent.com/pod-product-compliance
Lightning Source LLC
Chambersburg PA
CBHW042058040426
42448CB00002B/60